Designing Amusement Park Rides

by Michael A. DiSpezio

HOUGHTON MIFFLIN HARCOURT

PHOTOGRAPHY CREDITS: 4 (br) Comstock/Getty Images; 4 (bl) Photodisc/Getty Images; 5 (br) ©Digifoto Blue/Alamy Images; 6 (b) ©JUPITER IMAGES/Getty Images

Printed in Mexico

ISBN: 978-0-544-07291-6

4 5 6 7 8 9 10 0908 21 20 19 18 17 16

4500607998 A B C D E F G

Contents

Vocabulary

design process
experiment
communicate

Stretch Vocabulary

ride-show engineer
blueprint
variable
scale
inference

Introduction

Suppose you could design your own amusement-park ride. What might it look like? How fast would it go? Would it light up at night or perhaps make funny sounds?

Designing rides might not seem like a real job, but it is. People who design amusement-park rides are called ride-show engineers. To create a ride, these engineers follow the steps of the design process. When the process is complete, their idea has been developed into an actual ride.

Park rides look colorful and amusing, but they require careful engineering.

Rollercoasters

You may never have ridden a rollercoaster, but you've probably seen one. It is often the biggest, longest, and largest ride in an amusement park.

Rollercoasters vary in many different ways. In some rollercoasters, you ride in a car or compartment. In others, you sit on a seat as your feet hang in the air. Some rollercoasters have a spiral track that looks like a corkscrew. Others are on a track that dives straight down.

The Design Process

Suppose you were a ride-show engineer and had the chance to design your own rollercoaster. Where would you begin? You'd follow a basic design process.

The steps of the design process aren't fixed. They vary, depending upon what is being engineered. Also, engineers have identified different design processes. Which one is the right one to use? It depends on what you want to build and how you want to approach the project.

Designing a safe rollercoaster requires strong engineering skills.

Engineering and Society

Often the role of engineering is to meet a need in society. What products will improve our living conditions? How can we ensure a clean water supply? How can we build vehicles that use renewable resources?

Amusement parks help meet society's need to have fun. Engineers of rollercoasters and other park rides want to meet people's desire to safely experience thrills and excitement.

Researching a Project

Research is a very important part of the design process. You can learn about new designs and designs that didn't work, so you won't repeat the failures. Research can also inspire brand-new ideas.

Engineers can do research using professional journals and websites.

Like scientists, engineers publish essays about their work. These stories are found in special collections called journals. Journals offer all sorts of technical information about the latest findings.

A ride-show engineer may start by looking through a current journal. Journals may contain essays that suggest new and interesting designs.

Although information about older designs will be printed, information about newer ones will be in an electronic form, which can be found on CDs, DVDs, and the Internet.

The fun thing about researching amusement-park rides is that it also might involve visiting the parks. How cool is that?

The more you learn about rollercoasters, the more likely you'll be able to plan a successful project. But ride-show engineers must also do another type of research. They need to find out what types of rides people like. Do riders like sharp turns or steep drops? What makes a ride too scary? Ride designers can't afford to design an amusement-park ride that no one wants to go on.

Planning Your Design

Once engineers have a better idea of what they'd like to build, it's time to put ideas on paper. Engineers might begin with a drawing or a diagram. Each of these is a type of model. Engineers use models to try out designs.

The engineer must make specific decisions about the ride. How many hills will the rollercoaster have? Does the first hill have to be the highest? For now, it's okay to just put down thoughts. Later, the engineer will need to test the designs to uncover what works—and what doesn't.

There are all sorts of safety considerations. The ride needs to be safe! How sharp can the sharpest turn be? What braking system will keep the ride at a safe speed?

Diagrams are easy to change. At this point, engineers expect that the plan will keep changing. That's part of the design process. If engineers discover something that won't work on the actual ride, they have to change the design. The builders will use expensive materials, so it's much easier to make changes on paper.

Unless an engineer is using a giant sheet of paper, a diagram of a rollercoaster will be scaled down. It will look like the planned ride, but it will show a smaller version. However, it will have the same proportions.

One kind of diagram is called a blueprint. Blueprints are scale drawings of a design that include all necessary measurements. Blueprints include a scale that shows how to convert diagram measurements into those of the actual product. A scale might show a ratio of 1:100. That means one centimeter on the drawing is equal to 100 centimeters of the actual ride.

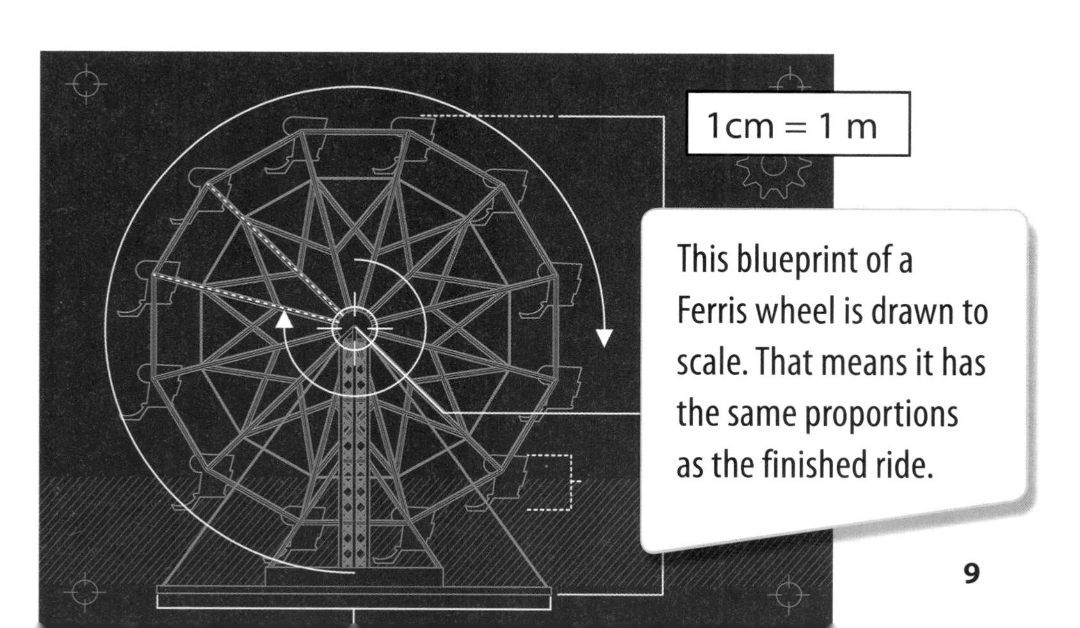

This blueprint of a Ferris wheel is drawn to scale. That means it has the same proportions as the finished ride.

Three-Dimensional Models

In addition to helping in the design process, models can be used to communicate a design to others. Three-dimensional models are especially good for this purpose. There are several different types of three-dimensional models to choose from, depending on what you need.

One type of model is a scale model. Although this model doesn't have to work, it communicates what the ride will look like once it's built.

A scale model might make an amusement park company want to buy your design. Many times, engineers must sell their design to an amusement park company before it can be built! That's why it's important to consider the construction costs.

Another type of model is a test model. A test model can also help engineers predict whether a design works. Often, a test model shows only a small part of the whole design. There's no need to build a model of the entire structure if you're only testing a part of it.

Thinking Like a Scientist

Testing is a form of scientific inquiry, a way of applying investigation and reasoning to answer questions and solve problems. Ride-show engineers ask all sorts of questions about their designs. How fast will the cars travel safely? How sharp can the curves be? Test models help engineers answer such questions.

In the past, engineers built most models out of the same materials used to construct the actual ride. Nowadays, however, modeling is often performed by computers. By using computer models, engineers can save time and money as they collect data.

Test models can show whether a design works before it is built.

Experiments and Variables

Engineers must follow the scientific approach when they peform experiments, even those done with a computer. To begin, they ask a question that focuses the investigation. Must the first hill be the highest? How does a car's weight affect its speed?

Engineers uncover the answers to questions like these using a controlled investigation. This means doing an experiment twice.

First, the experiment is performed and the data collected. The second time, everything except one element or condition, called a variable, remains the same. The experimental variable is changed. Then, the experiment is repeated.

If the results are the same, then changing the variable had no effect. If the results are different, then the variable affected the outcome. That's the scientific approach! You now have a hard fact to work with.

When collecting data, it's important to know the difference between facts and inferences. An inference is a logical conclusion you reach based on the evidence. If you see a friend with a baseball standing next to a broken window, you might infer she broke it. You're probably right, but you could be wrong. Further investigation could turn this inference into a fact.

Experimental variables are often used to find out why something isn't working.

The Final Test

At first you feel a slight jolt. The car lurches ahead. Then the ride smoothes out. Moving out from under the canopy, you face upward into the blue sky. Slowly and steadily the car climbs.

The ride has already passed safety and performance tests. This is the final, and most important, test of the engineer's design. Will passengers like the ride?

The final test of the design: Is the ride fun?

Responding

Make a Scale Drawing

Think of a design for something you would like to build, like a tree house. Then make a scale drawing of the thing to be built. Try to include all the information that someone would need to carry out your design. Add to your drawing a scale showing the exact ratio you are using. For example, your scale might look like this:

2 cm = 1 m

Describe a Process

Write down the steps someone would need to follow in order to build the thing you designed for your scale drawing. Make sure that the steps are in the correct order. Be careful not to leave any important steps out. Include any necessary safety procedures a builder would need to follow. Number the steps and give your description a title.

Glossary

blueprint [BLOO•print] A scale drawing of a thing used to help build it.

communicate [kuh•MYOO•nih•KAYT] To give or receive information.

design process [dih•ZYN PRAHS•es] The process of applying basic principles of engineering to solve problems.

experiment [ek•SPAIR•uh•muhnt] A test done to see whether a hypothesis is correct.

inference [IN•fer•uhns] An untested conclusion based on your observations.

ride-show engineer [RYD•shoh en•juh•NIR] An engineer applies scientific and mathematical principles to develop something practical. A ride-show engineer is an engineer who develops rides for amusement parks.

scale [SKAYL] A type of drawing or diagram that shows something as smaller in size but having the same proportions.

variable [VAIR•ee•uh•buhl] In a controlled investigation, a variable is the part of an experiment that is changed from one trial to the next.